Theology of the Body Made Simple

Theology of the Body Made Simple

Anthony Percy

Foreword by Professor Kenneth Schmitz

BOOKS & MEDIA
Boston

Library of Congress Cataloging-in-Publication Data

Percy, Anthony.
  Theology of the body made simple / Anthony Percy.— 1st North American ed.
    p. cm.
  Includes bibliographical references.
  ISBN 0-8198-7419-1 (pbk. : alk. paper) 1. Sex—Religious aspects—Catholic Church. 2. Body, Human—Religious aspects—Catholic Church. 3. John Paul II, Pope, 1920-2005. Theology of the body. 4. Catholic Church—Doctrines. I. Title.
  BX1795.S48P45 2006
  233'.5—dc22

                              2006002785

Bible quotations, unless otherwise noted, are from the *Revised Standard Version of the Bible,* copyright 1946, 1952, 1971 by the Division of Christian Education of the National Council of Churches of Christ.

Excerpts from the English translation of the *Catechism of the Catholic Church* for use in the United States of America, copyright © 1994, United States Catholic Conference, Inc. – Libreria Editrice Vaticana. Used with Permission.

Cover design by Rosana Usselmann

Cover photo Dougal / Waters / Getty Images

Original edition published under the title *Theology of the Body Made Simple* by Connor Court Publishing, Ballan, Victoria, Australia, (www.connorcourt.com.au).

First North American Edition, 2006

Published by Pauline Books & Media, 50 Saint Paul's Avenue, Boston, MA 02130-3491. www.pauline.org.

Printed in the U.S.A.

Pauline Books & Media is the publishing house of the Daughters of St. Paul, an international congregation of women religious serving the Church with the communications media.

1 2 3 4 5 6 7 8 9   11 10 09 08 07 06

Contents

Foreword

Father Anthony Percy has given us a map that marks out guideposts in John Paul II's *Theology of the Body,* while at the same time he presents us with a plain, clear volume with a value of its own. He has done this by alerting us to the keys that open the first part of the text from which the rest of John Paul II's work follows.

These keys are experiences that, with the light of the faith, are accessible to the deepest part of our lives. They are deepest because they take us back to "the beginning" revealed to us in the Bible's Book of Genesis. Fr. Percy describes them with brevity and a freshness that is original yet faithful to John Paul's insights, and that can draw us into the heart of the late pope's thought. These experiences belong to humanity's beginning, but not exclusively to that time of prehistory, for "with the aid of revelation" we also recognize them as part of *our* experience in these latter days.

There are four pillars of human experience, and they manifest four fundamental qualities of the human body. I will only name them here and let you, the reader, discover them for yourself in this book. They are all "originals": Original Solitude, Original Unity, Original Nakedness, and, alas!, all too familiar: Original Sin. Father Percy unfolds these and, with examples and vivid images, gives color to the text in an easy-to-understand, conversational style.

Following from these original experiences are four qualities of the human body. The *symbolic* quality of the body shows forth the invisible interiority of the person. From this flows an insight into the very nature of language itself and the intimate and gracious presence of words in our communication with each other. It is language rooted in the word given to us from the Father. The Book of Genesis reveals the other qualities as well: the *nuptial* character of the body, but also a *freedom* that is *fallen* and a freedom that, in Jesus Christ, is *redeemed*. Having these qualities is not simply a condition of the body, but an experience that, through revelation, is at the root of every human experience.

Who would have thought that there could be "new discoveries about the human body" in the third millennium? John Paul II's profound insights, and Father Percy's down-to-earth explanation, are enough to invite us to a new sense of what it means to be a human person and a child of God.

KENNETH SCHMITZ

Preface

The *Theology of the Body* is a rather intriguing name given to a collection of teachings offered by Pope John Paul II. John Paul was elected to the papacy in 1978 and began to present the *Theology of the Body* in 1979, finishing it five years later in 1984. *Some* teaching! *Theology of the Body Made Simple*—as the name suggests—attempts to simplify what at times can be a very difficult and complex topic. I hope that I am successful. You be the judge.

Only in recent times have people begun to appreciate the significance of the *Theology of the Body*. There are probably many reasons for this—we need not go into them here. Let it suffice to say that many people, especially the young, have shown considerable interest in this new teaching and have found it fascinating and challenging.

The *Theology of the Body* is a new teaching about:

✧ The human body and human sexuality;
✧ Human relationships;

✧   Marriage and celibacy (the single life).

The teaching views these three realities as God would view them, that is, in the light of faith. For this reason, I would say the *Theology of the Body* is essentially about the *meaning of life*. This will become clear after you read chapter one.

The *Theology of the Body* has much to say about human sexuality, but it is fundamentally a teaching on human relationships and how these relationships are a reflection of God himself. Sexuality is part and parcel of our lives. Human beings—males and females—are deeply sexual creatures. We know from experience that the sexual urge is powerful. We don't need textbooks or manuals to tell us this.

> The desire to be loved and to love is much deeper than the desire to have sex.

But according to John Paul II, we are more *relational* than we are *sexual*. Let's put it this way: the desire to be loved and to love is much deeper than the desire to have sex. The pope is quite insistent on this point. Sex is a wonderful reality. But at the same time it is a means to an end. Sex is supposed to serve fruitful, lasting relationships and is therefore subservient to marriage and celibacy's higher value.

John Paul teaches that the human body is profoundly relational. We reach perfection through relationships. We are called to associate with others, accept others, affirm others, give ourselves to others, forgive others, etc. In short, we are called to love and to accept love. We are called to develop intimate and enduring friendships on earth; these very friendships are an intimation of the true and definitive friendship Jesus Christ offers to us.

This does not mean, however, that everyone is necessarily called to have sex. Let me paraphrase the pope's words. The pope says that *our bodies and our sexuality are not exactly the same thing. Man is a body, and this belongs to him as a human person more deeply than whether his body is male or female.*

Sexuality is essential. No one can deny it. In fact, John Paul II emphatically affirms sex perhaps more than any other pope in history. But—and this is the pope's precise point—sexuality should serve a true and lasting communion between men and women, between husband and wife. Indeed, sex should bring us into a true and lasting communion with God. This is so because God is a communion of persons. God is Father, Son, and Holy Spirit living a life of love, and we are the images of God.

Love, then, takes precedence over sexual activity, which is why celibate people and those contemplating the celibate vocation will find great encouragement in the pope's teaching. By the end of chapter two, therefore, I hope you will be able to see that God has created us with a view to relationships with each other and with himself.

Chapter three deals with sexuality and sexual acts. I have attempted to apply Pope John Paul's teaching to particular sexual activities. You will find no deviation from the Church's traditional sexual teaching, but hopefully you will discover new, more reasonable, and more satisfying reasons for the teaching. Once again, you be the judge as to whether I have succeeded.

The Church's sexual teaching can *develop*—and has *developed*—over time. But it has not *changed*—and will not *change*—over time. In his *Theology of the Body*, Pope John Paul II has expanded the Church's teaching with respect to marriage, celibacy, and sexuality. He has brought fresh insights into how we understand the mystery of the human body and sexuality.

In fact, in presenting the *Theology of the Body*, John Paul was following the lead of Pope John XXIII, who in 1962, in what became known as the Second Vatican Council, called the world's bishops together to deepen their understanding of the nature of the Church and her relationship with the world. Even back then, John XXIII noted that the truths of Christianity never change, but that the way these truths are expressed and presented can and must change.

So, on the one hand, the Church must remain faithful to Christ and his teaching. What would happen if the Church attempted to change or alter the teaching of Christ? What kind of a Church would that be? The simple answer is *unfaithful*. On the other hand, the teaching must be expressed in a language that modern men and women can understand. What would happen if the Church used language foreign to her members and the world at large? What kind of a Church would that be? The simple answer is *irrelevant*.

I hope, therefore, that upon reading *Theology of the Body Made Simple*, you will find encouragement in following the Church's teaching on sexuality. Furthermore, and just as important, I hope this book gives you a *language* that will enable you to talk to your friends about the deeper issues of life. Many people today are genuinely confused about the meaning of life, human relationships, and sexuality. The *Theology of the Body* can help them and become a foundation stone for future generations.

Quite a few people have helped me with this book. I thank them for their generosity. Of special note is Father John Riccardo from the Archdiocese of Detroit. We studied together at the John Paul II Institute for Studies in Marriage and Family in Washington, D.C. There we were able to take some time together to digest the pope's thoughts. His suggestions have been very helpful.

Introduction

The *Theology of the Body* is a new and fresh approach to the human body and to sexual morality. *Theos* is the Greek word for "God," and *logos* is Greek for "word." Theology, therefore, is "a word about God," or the study of God. Theology is also the study of all created things. God is light, says St. John. The light of God shines upon our minds and hearts, giving us a clear vision of God himself and all that God has made. John Paul II has studied the human body, therefore, with the aid of the light God grants us.

Normally we are accustomed to think of and study the human body from other angles. For instance, we can study the human body from the perspective of health, biology, physics, chemistry, and even economics. These approaches are useful. But when studied and considered in isolation, they tend to be incomplete. They need to be understood in a wider and more generous context so that the truth of the human body may shine forth. The pope does this, in a new way, by study-ing the human body from God's perspective.

Method and Content

What is the method and content of this new approach? John Paul II has a simple method. The pope starts with the Word of God. He relies heavily on the Book of Genesis, the first book of the Bible. Then he introduces and uses human experience to develop his teaching. As we will see, the Bible and human experi-ence go together well.

The content of the Theology of the Body has two parts, with three chapters in each part.

PART ONE
The Words of Christ

CHAPTER ONE
Christ Appeals to the Beginning

CHAPTER TWO
Christ Appeals to the Human Heart

CHAPTER THREE
Christ Appeals to the Resurrection

PART TWO
The Sacrament

CHAPTER ONE
The Dimension of Covenant and of Grace

CHAPTER TWO

The Dimension of Sign

CHAPTER THREE

He Gave Them the Law of Life as Their Inheritance*

Because everything else flows from it, I will focus exclusively on chapter one of the first part of the *Theology of the Body*. In this first part, the pope develops four original experiences and then goes on to develop four qualities of the human body. This is the fundamental content of the *Theology of the Body* teaching, and it is quite extraordinary. Once you grasp the content of this very first chapter, you will be able to read and comprehend the rest of the pope's teaching.

There are four chapters in this book. Chapter one looks at the original human experiences. Chapter two examines the qualities of the human body. Chapter three discusses sexual morality, and chapter four speaks about the mercy and forgiveness of Jesus Christ. Reading the chapters in order will help you understand the topic better.

---

* This division of the parts of the *Theology of the Body* is based on John Paul II's original Polish manuscript, recently discovered in the John Paul II Archives and published in the new translation of *The Theology of the Body* (Michael M. Waldstein, trans. Boston: Pauline Books & Media, 2006 [www.pauline.org]).

When and Where Did the Pope Give This New Teaching?

The pope taught the *Theology of the Body* from September 5, 1979, to November 28, 1984. People who come to Rome to visit the ancient city often want to catch a glimpse of the pope. One way of doing this is to get a ticket to what is called a "Wednesday audience" in St. Peter's Square. People assemble, and the pope comes out to give a brief talk, bless them, show them his love, and encourage them in their Christian lives. Pope John Paul II used these occasions to teach us about the meaning of the human body and sexuality.

Why the New Teaching and Approach?

A famous Catholic writer, G. K. Chesterton, wrote in the 1920s that there was *more madness coming out of Manhattan than Moscow*. In 1917 the Communist Revolution had taken place in Russia. But another revolution was erupting. It was, and is, more subtle and, in a sense, far more dangerous. Chesterton was referring to the sexual revolution. It was underway back in the 1920s, and he foresaw that it would present an enormous challenge to society.

Can there be any doubt that Chesterton was right? In London, a recent study of nine thousand students with an average age of thirteen found that one in every fourteen of those surveyed had had sex by age thirteen.

Interestingly, 36 percent of the girls and 32 percent of the boys regretted their loss of virginity.

As we look around and witness the enormous pain and suffering caused by broken marriages and sexual promiscuity, there can be little doubt that we have a problem. As a father of four teenage children said to me recently, "They are taking our kids off the shelf, and the kids are not being put back on it."

Of course these problems are not new. Sexuality is a paradox. It is a marvelous but difficult reality. Yet difficulties and problems are good for us. Problems present a challenge—an opportunity. We are, therefore, living in a *favorable time*. We can try something new. This is what John Paul II has done with his *Theology of the Body*.

In times past the Church simply stated her sexual teaching. She always taught that sex before marriage, masturbation, adultery, contraception, deviant sexual fantasies, etc., were sinful and harmful acts. Popes, bishops, priests, nuns, and parents would speak the truth on sexual issues. People were simply asked to trust the teaching without a lot of explanation. This worked when an atmosphere of trust prevailed in the Church and in society in general. But since the 1960s and the "age of liberation," this approach has proved quite unsuccessful. People now view most institutions—especially the Church—with a good deal of suspicion. Clearly, our time calls for a new approach.

In addition, in times past the sexual teaching of the Church was not always presented positively. On many occasions, it was conveyed simply as a series of imperatives beginning with the words "don't do this." Positive reasons why people should not sleep together before marriage or look at pornography, for instance, were not always forthcoming; promoting the fear of sexual sin was the main tool the Church had at her disposal. It was effective to some extent, but now this approach does not carry much weight.

John Paul II addressed these critical concerns with his *Theology of the Body*. He introduces us into a new understanding of the human body and sexuality. His approach is positive, reasonable, and conversational.

Sex Is Important

Helping people—particularly teenagers, young adults, and young married couples—see the truth of sexuality is a priority. Helping people enter marriage as virgins is important. The Bible says we are temples of the Holy Spirit—and sin, including sexual sin, attacks that reality. Sexuality is an important matter. TV, movies, and magazines confirm this; in a sense, they are obsessed with it. Sex matters; it is an important dimension of our lives. No one can deny it.

But where does sex fit into our lives? What values are associated with it? Is it intimate and sacred? Or is it

simply "a casual indoor sport"? Pope John Paul II believes that sex means something. But the pope is not reacting to the sexual revolution; rather, he is responding to it. Remember that the rev- olution began quite some

> **Where does sex fit into our lives?**

time ago, and the Church is like everyone else: she needed time to think things through and reflect on the real causes of the problem. This is what John Paul II has done.

How to Understand the Church's Sexual Teaching

This book is not a textbook. If you are looking for a textbook, then you could consult the following books: *The Christian Meaning of Human Sexuality* by Father Paul Quay, S.J.; *The Catechism of the Catholic Church; Love and Responsibility* by Karol Wojtyla (Pope John Paul II); and a document by Pope Paul VI called *Humanae Vitae.* An excellent book on the broader questions of morality, faith, sacraments, and prayer is *Catholic Christianity: A Complete Catechism of Catholic Beliefs based on the Catechism of the Catholic Church* by Peter Kreeft. A comprehensive study of John Paul II's *Theology of the Body* can be found in *Theology of the Body Explained* by Christopher West (Boston: Pauline Books & Media, 2003 [www.pauline.org]). And, of course, don't forget the primary text written by Pope John Paul II, *The Theology of the Body* (Michael M. Waldstein, trans. Boston: Pauline Books & Media, 2006 [www.pauline.org]).

Of particular note is the document *Humanae Vitae* ("Of Human Life"). Pope Paul VI wrote it in 1968, and it caused quite a stir. It is well known for its opposition to artificial contraception. *Humanae Vitae* is about that and much more. It is short and easy to read, but many people who find aspects of the Church's teaching on sexuality difficult have never had the opportunity to read Pope Paul's booklet. Upon reading it they often experience a change of heart. Try reading it. You can find it on the worldwide web. Just search for *Humanae Vitae*.* These resources, and hopefully this book, will provide a good introduction to sexuality. In addition, a discussion group with friends might be a good way to facilitate understanding.

---

* Also available as a booklet from Pauline Books & Media (www.pauline.org).

Chapter One

The Original
Human Experience

Some people have called the *Theology of the Body* a "revolution." George Weigel, author of *Witness to Hope*, a biography of Pope John Paul II, claims that the *Theology of the Body* is a "theological time bomb waiting to go off." In this chapter, I will outline the basic method the pope uses in his *Theology of the Body*. Then I will introduce the four original experiences Pope John Paul II develops. You are probably already familiar with Original Sin, but you may not have heard of the other three original experiences. These three other original experiences constitute part of the "theological time bomb." In chapter two we will discover the other parts of the "time bomb" when we examine the qualities of the human body. Now let's look at how the pope develops his *Theology of the Body* and follow his method.

The Bible and Human Experience

In the *Theology of the Body*, the pope makes extensive use of the Bible and human experience. First, he uses the Bible, which is the word of God. God actually speaks to us in many ways. Above all, he speaks through his Son, Jesus Christ. The four Gospels tell us about Jesus' life. In addition—and this is important—they make Christ present to us now, in the twenty-first century.

When we read the Bible, we are not just reading a historical book. We are reading something much more dynamic, something that is putting us into actual living contact with Jesus Christ. So when we read of the death of Christ, we are mysteriously present at that event. Christ is really dying for us now. Therefore, in the Bible, he speaks to us now. Read the Bible this way, and it will change your life. Read it like any other history book, and you will miss the point completely.

Second, John Paul II relies on human experience. The Bible and experience go together. For instance, we are asked: "How do we know Jesus Christ?" We answer: "We know him through the Bible and through personal experience." We read the Bible and experience Jesus in prayer—he is real and living. He is like no other.

In addition, we experience him in and through our friends, family, teachers, sports, work, nature, etc. If we are Catholic, we experience him in the community of the Church and in the sacraments. In the Eucharist we literally eat his body and drink his blood. In all these ways we experience the crucified and risen Jesus Christ. Experience is important for John Paul II. We will see this as we read and discover his *Theology of the Body*.

"The Beginning"

Let's start with the Bible. John Paul II begins with this passage from the Gospel of Matthew 19:3–12.

> And Pharisees came up to him and tested him by asking, "Is it lawful to divorce one's wife for any cause?" He answered, "Have you not read that he who made them from the beginning made them male and female, and said, 'for this reason a man shall leave his father and mother and be joined to his wife, and the two shall become one flesh'? So they are no longer two but one flesh. What therefore God has joined together, let not man put asunder." They said to him, "Why then did Moses command one to give a certificate of divorce, and to put her away?" He said to them, "For your hardness of heart Moses allowed you to divorce your wives, but from *the beginning* it was not so. And I say to you: whoever divorces his wife, except for unchastity, and marries another, commits adultery; and he who marries a divorced woman commits adultery."
>
> The disciples said to him, "If such is the case of a man with his wife, it is not expedient to marry." But he said to them, "Not all men can receive this saying, but only those to whom it is given. For there are

eunuchs who have been so from birth, and there are eunuchs who have been made eunuchs by men, and there are eunuchs who have made themselves eunuchs for the sake of the kingdom of heaven. He who is able to receive this, let him receive it."

When Jesus spoke these words, divorce was common. Jesus' words surprised the disciples, and they surprise us also. Remember, too, that marriage was not common in the Roman Empire. The marriage rate was so low that on several occasions Roman emperors decreed that men should marry. Roman men preferred to stay single and enjoy a life without commitment. In addition, abortion was common, as was infanticide, contraception, and homosexuality. The world at the time of Christ, and at the time of the early Church, was not unlike ours.

> The world at the time of Christ, and at the time of the early Church, was not unlike ours. Yet Christ did not hesitate to speak the truth.

Yet Christ did not hesitate to speak the truth. In fact, in responding to the Pharisees' question, Jesus raises the stakes. He speaks not only of marriage, but also of celibacy—something virtually unheard-of in the ancient world. He speaks of it as accepting a gift given. Some people will be asked to live a celibate life;

they will feel the call of God to forsake all, follow him, and be totally free to build his kingdom. This, too, surprised the disciples and also surprises us.

I have highlighted the phrase "the beginning" in Jesus' reply. What is "the beginning"? It is described in the first book of the Bible, the Book of Genesis 1:1, 27: "In *the beginning*...male and female [God] created them." So "the beginning" means the creation of man and woman. But it also means more.

Jesus immediately goes on to quote from Genesis 2:24: "Therefore a man leaves his father and his mother and cleaves to his wife, and they become one flesh." God created Adam and Eve with the intention that they would become "one flesh." God created them with a view to an intimate unity whereby they would share their very lives.

To reflect more on this idea of intention, think of many of our common activities. A person turns on the computer and makes a new file to write a letter for a job application. Or perhaps he or she is writing a paper for high school or college. People start out with a purpose—with an intention. This is exactly what God does with us. In the Bible this intention or purpose is referred to as "the beginning."

God creates us with an intention in mind. In the passage cited above, Jesus reveals to us his Father's intention: men and women are called to be either married or celibate. Either way, the call is a gift from God.

Most people are called to be "one flesh" with a person of the opposite sex. Others—a few—are called to be celibate. But in both cases—marriage or celibacy—the calling is a gift from God.

Neither marriage nor celibacy is something we humans invented. Rather, God gives us marriage and celibacy as a gift. Many people today have never heard of such an idea, or perhaps they have forgotten it. Either way, it is our privilege to introduce the idea or remind them of it.

The "Theological Time Bomb" Explodes!

Before I explain the four original experiences, let's stop here to recognize the "theological time bomb" that the *Theology of the Body* contains. Suppose we are asked to complete this phrase: "Original _____." What do we answer? My guess is that we, and most people who have received an adequate Christian education, would respond: "Original Sin."

With Pope John Paul II's *Theology of the Body*, the response is radically different. The response becomes:

Original Solitude;
Original Unity;
Original Nakedness;
Original Sin.

Pope John Paul II does not want to deny the truth and reality of Original Sin. That would be absurd. But he wants to take us back to "the beginning"—to what God intended. John Paul II wants to take us back before Original Sin existed. He wants to do this precisely because Jesus Christ took us back to "the beginning." Only in this way can we see the real meaning of human life and human sexuality.

So using the first two chapters of the Book of Genesis, the pope develops three original human experiences called Original Solitude, Original Unity, and Original Nakedness. These occur before Original Sin. The important point for us to remember is this: we, too, have access to these original experiences precisely because Christ grants it to us. We are already familiar with the experience of Original Sin. We have had, and will continue to have, an experience of failure and sin. But now in the *Theology of the Body*, Pope John Paul II makes it clear that we can have the positive experiences of Solitude, Unity, and Nakedness, too.

Having these positive experiences is precisely what Christ wants us to do. He wants to take us back to "the beginning" so we can discover the real meaning of the human body and human sexuality—i.e., the meaning of life. Herein lies the "theological time bomb." Christians know the reality of Original Sin, but they have not been given a vivid awareness, through a rich and penetrating catechesis, of the experiences that occurred *before* Original Sin. By taking us back to "the beginning," Christ desires to give this to us, and his desire is now expressed through Pope John Paul II. He desires that, like Adam and Eve, we will have the experiences of *Solitude*, *Unity*, and *Nakedness*. This truly can spark a revolution.

> In the beginning, we were not broken, but whole. Thus our relationships with each other were also peaceful and intimate.

What, then, do we find happening before Original Sin? We find two chapters in the Book of Genesis in which God and humanity are on *intimate* terms. In other words, we experienced a great peace with God, and our relationship with him was intimate and true. Furthermore, we knew ourselves intimately, and we experienced ourselves as integral people. We were not broken, but whole. Thus our relationships with each other were also peaceful and intimate. By going back to "the beginning," we can see what God intended and had in fact established at the beginning of time. This is how John Paul II develops the four original experiences.

To develop the first three experiences of Original Solitude, Original Unity, and Original Nakedness, John Paul II focuses on Genesis 2:15–25. (Take a close look at the italicized words.)

The LORD God took the man and put him in the garden of Eden to till it and keep it. And the LORD God commanded the man, saying, "You may freely eat of every tree of the garden; but of the tree of the knowledge of good and evil you shall not eat, for in the day that you eat of it you shall die." Then the LORD God said, "It is not good that the man should be alone; I will make him a *helper* fit for him." So out of the ground the LORD God formed every beast of the field and every bird of the air, and *brought them* to the man to see what he would *call* them; and whatever the man called every living creature, that was its name. The man gave names to all cattle, and to the birds of the air, and to every beast of the field; but for the man there was *not found a helper* fit for him. So the LORD God caused a deep sleep to fall upon the man, and while he slept took one of his ribs and closed up its place with flesh; and the rib which the LORD God had taken from the man he made into a woman and *brought her to the man*. Then the man said, "*This at last is bone of my bones and flesh of my flesh*; she shall be called Woman, because she was taken out of Man." Therefore a man leaves his father and his mother and *cleaves* to his wife, and they become *one flesh*. And the man and his wife were both *naked*, and were *not ashamed*.

Original Solitude

The Bible contains two accounts of creation. The first one is Genesis 1:1–3. The second account is Genesis 2:4–24, and it begins where the first account ends.

Genesis 1 and Genesis 2 have different perspectives because different people wrote them. But they both teach the same truth: namely, that God created the world and humanity out of nothing. Read them to see the difference. Remember, however, that they are not written like history. After all, when God created the world, no one was around to see it.

Rather than history, in the first two chapters of Genesis we find writing that is like the writing in the Wisdom Books of the Old Testament. This wisdom comes to us in literary forms that are more like poetry. After many years of experiencing God, the Chosen People were able to reflect on God's creative power. Eventually they committed these things to writing under the influence of the Holy Spirit, who taught them in and through their experience. The first two chapters of Genesis, therefore, contain religious truths in the form of poetry that utilizes all sorts of techniques to communicate profound truths. Let's stop and think about this. We often use metaphors and comparisons in recounting an event. Someone gets embarrassed, or someone gets angry about something. In retelling the story we say to a friend: "You should have seen John. He was as red as a beet." Somehow this expression communicates more of the truth than if we were to say simply: "John was angry" or "John was embarrassed."

The Bible does this, too. It uses a wide range of literary techniques and devices to communicate the truth of

God and how he relates with us. Some of the books of the Old Testament are more like history books. This is true, for instance, for most of the Book of Genesis, excluding the first three chapters. Some are prophetic books, like Isaiah and Daniel. Others, like the Book of Jonah, are satires. So the Scriptures contain many books that are written in various and different ways. But they all communicate the truth. Failure to recognize this will turn us into fundamentalists, and then we won't understand what God is trying to say to us.

With this in mind, let's return to Original Solitude. John Paul II focuses on the second account of creation, as cited above. Let's take a look at those highlighted sections. First, notice the passage mentions the word "God" six times. This indicates that the man could sense God and his presence. God and the man were friends: they could talk and listen to each other; they were familiar with each other.

Second, the man is different from the other creatures in the Garden. The man is given a special responsibility: God actually brings the animals to the man and asks him to name them. In the Bible, naming means knowing the creatures and having dominion over them—a bit like God knowing us. Notice what happens in the scene. The man sees and names all the creatures God creates, but none of them is like him. He does not find a bodily creature that is the same as himself. The man realizes this and begins to understand that, while he has a body like all of the other creatures, his body is different.

Let's see what Original Solitude means from these initial observations. It means two things. First, the man is alone with God and enjoys a unique relationship with God. So while God created all the other animals in the Garden just as he created the man, only the man is able to talk and listen to God. God speaks with us in a totally unique way. We are different from the animals. This is the first meaning of Original Solitude. We are uniquely alone with God—we stand before God. We are in the presence of God.

> We are uniquely alone with God—we stand before God. We are in the presence of God.

This means that, unlike animals, we relate directly to God. We can carry on a conversation with him. We have a spirit that enables us to do this, and by it we can know and love God, the world, and ourselves. This should come as no surprise to us. As human beings we can know and understand things. In a certain way, so can some creatures. For instance, a dog can know some things, but it has a very limited knowledge.

In addition, however, we as human beings *know that we know*. We are conscious that we know; we can reflect on events and our knowledge of them. Once again, let's stop and reflect on our own rich experience of life, as the pope wants us to do. We work at our jobs or go to school, we have hobbies, we play sports, we form relationships, and we do a host of other things. As we do these things we grow in our knowledge. But then we also, at various times, reflect on our behavior—on our lives. We become conscious of knowing things and realize how we have developed as persons. This is Original Solitude. It is unique to us as human beings. Through this fundamental, or original, experience, we come to sense the uniqueness of human life. We realize that we are able to know God, the world (especially other people), and ourselves. In other words, we begin to realize our personal identities.

Original Solitude has a second meaning. While realizing his uniqueness, the man notices that *something is wrong*. Actually, God notices it first! God says, "It is not good that the man should be alone." Yet, in knowing and naming all the animals, the man did not find another body like his. He was alone. This second meaning of Original Solitude is different from the first. The first is more positive. Through the first experience, the man knows his special place in creation. The second experience is negative. The man sees that there is no one around like him—a bit like being on a deserted island. Something is lacking in his life.

Original Unity

To remedy that lack, God gets to work. He places Adam in a deep sleep, and Adam awakens to discover another being. He notices a body that is like his. More, he notices that this body, while similar, is different from his. And he realizes *she* is a person. Furthermore, the man decides to be one with the woman. He leaves his former life and becomes one flesh with her. This is Original Unity. A man finds his perfection—his fulfillment—not in a solitary life, but in a unified life with a woman. Adam has made a second discovery. Not only is he alone with God, but now he is alone with another unique being. He has a partner with whom he is alone, and together they are alone with God.

Our experience, too, teaches us this truth. Haven't there been times when despite doing well in our lives (studies, work, career, etc.), we felt something was missing? That something is being with others. We call it friendship, companionship, and intimacy. The Bible tells us that friendship is like the air that we breathe. Without friendship, we perish.

> A faithful friend is a sturdy shelter:
> he that has found one has found a treasure.
> There is nothing so precious as a faithful friend,
> and no scales can measure his excellence.
> A faithful friend is an elixir of life;
> and those who fear the LORD will find him.
> (Sir 6:14–16)

What do the experiences of Original Solitude and Original Unity mean for us? They mean that God created us to be in relationship with him and with other human beings. We are *created to be related*. Why would this be so? Because God himself is a related being.

God is the Father, Son, and Holy Spirit. God is the Father loving the Son and the Son loving the Father. The love between them is so intense and real that this love is, in fact, another person—the Holy Spirit. While being three distinct persons, God is in fact a profound unity. God the Father, the Son, and Holy Spirit are distinct but inseparable.

We are created in the image and likeness of God. Human beings are like God. We are distinct, but inseparable. We are related-beings. Relationship is the name of the game. It is what life is about. The experiences of Original Solitude and Original Unity confirm this.

By now we can see what is happening. By going back to "the beginning" we start to get a glimpse of God's intention, or desire, for us. Through the words of the first book of the Bible we are coming to understand the truth of who we are as human beings. In other words, by going back to the "beginning" we understand the mystery and truth of who we are.

God is showing us this step by step. Notice how this differs from other fields of study. If we study humanity through biology, chemistry, physics, medicine, economics, law, etc., we will get some answers. But we will only get partial answers. If we want the full answer about humanity, then we must pay close attention to what God tells us. Only he will tell us the full truth about humanity. Then we can fit the other sciences into this vision. Many people do not appreciate this and end up with distorted views about humanity.

In the second original experience, Original Unity, Adam awakes from the divine sleep to find that God has been at work fashioning Eve. Adam sees her and is really delighted. "At last," he says, "bone of my bones and flesh of my flesh." Adam notices two things about this new creature. She is the same, but different. She is human, to be sure, but she looks different. She is a woman. Adam is immediately attracted to her. We are told that henceforth man will leave father and mother and cleave to his wife. The man and the woman, we are told, become "one flesh."

Have we not experienced the same reality? As young boys or young girls, we find that our attraction to the opposite sex is not strong. But suddenly, in the years following puberty, we feel more attracted to the opposite sex. A whole new world opens up for us. If you are a man, the body of a woman delights and attracts you. Her body is different. Men say, on seeing a woman, "Isn't she beautiful!" And women say, on seeing a man, "Isn't he handsome!" This attraction is good. God desires it—it is perfectly normal and holy.

All this enables us to see the deep connection between Original Solitude and Original Unity. On the one hand, Adam experiences that he is unique in creation: he is alone with God like no other creature is. On the other hand, his experience tells him that something is lacking in his life. He knows that despite being alone with God, he still needs someone else: a woman. He feels alone. With the help of God he searches for this other. In fact, the biblical text says God himself presents the woman to the man. In effect, God is saying, "This is my daughter—care for her, love her!" Adam accepts Eve. He becomes one with her; they become one flesh.

Let's be more precise. What is the essence of Original Unity? John Paul II says it consists in two things: accepting and giving. The man discovers the woman and *accepts* her for who she is. The man does not try to change her or control her. The man accepts that she complements him—that she helps him to be human.

Recall what God says in the Book of Genesis: "It is not good that man should be alone; I will make him a helper fit for him." The word "helper" is used twenty-one times in the Old Testament. Nineteen times it refers to divine aid. The woman, then, is a divine aid, not "merely" a helper (which can sound disparaging). The woman lifts the man beyond himself; she helps him reach perfection. This is so precisely because the woman complements the man. Of course the reverse is true as well; the man helps the woman attain her perfection.

Remember that the man and the woman are the same, but they are also different. John Paul II says man and woman are two different incarnations of the human person. Incarnation is a word that means *made flesh*. So the man and the woman are truly human persons; they love, think, and remember, and they do all this in and through their human bodies.

A person has a will, intellect, and memory. These are spiritual realities. But these realities are differently expressed in men and women. These differences manifest themselves not only in how men and women think, act, and love. The difference is also expressed in the way they look—their bodily appearance.

The bodily difference is obvious to us, yet studies confirm the profound spiritual difference that exists, too. Years ago a book called *Brain Sex* documented some of these differences. Apparently, if you ask a little boy and a little girl to look at an image, they will notice entirely different things. For instance, the little girl will notice the people and the relationships in the scene, whereas the little boy will observe the objects in the scene. Again, little girls speak with words approximately 100 percent of the time, while little boys use words only 70 percent of the time—the rest of the time they use noises to communicate.

People who have worked extensively in marriage education and counseling suggest that women tend to be more relational than men. Men tend to be more goal or task orientated. Confirming this intuition and observation, recent studies have found that on average men speak around ten thousand words per day and women speak around twenty-five thousand words per day.

What do we make of the differences? Should we accept them or try to alter them? No doubt some minor changes could be made. For instance, those who work extensively with married couples note that a woman's strength lies in her ability to relate. However, she can become controlling in her relationships. At times, too, she can become compulsive or obsessive. A man's strength, on the other hand, lies in his ability to be a leader. Men like to achieve results. Hence, they like to be respected. But men can become irresponsible and easily abandon their responsibilities.

We can all make improvements as we mature and develop. This is part of what makes us human. But for the most part, the differences between men and women should be respected, accepted, and enhanced. They are God-given realities, and thus they are good. Men and women should be accepted for what they are: different ways of being a human being.

So Adam looks upon Eve and not only notices her obvious physical differences, but also begins to realize her profound spiritual differences. As a consequence, he is attracted to her. Because she complements him, Adam can become "one flesh" with Eve. Adam accepts Eve. In fact, Adam rejoices in Eve. Her beauty attracts him forcefully. But at the same time, Adam *gives* himself to Eve and the two of them become one flesh. This is the second dimension of Original Unity. Adam is entranced by Eve, but he is not forced to be one with her. Rather, Adam wants to be one with her, and so he gives himself to her. He uses his freedom and chooses Eve as his lifetime partner. He cleaves to her. He and his wife have begun a new life. It is a new life in which Adam gives himself to Eve and accepts Eve completely. Likewise, Eve is living a new life. It, too, is one of acceptance and giving.

These two realities—accepting and giving—form the basis of any true friendship. John Paul II says this *experience of unity* is truly significant because both Adam and Eve gain a new sense of their own dignity. They feel and experience life in a new way. They experience themselves in a new way. This radical experience of giving and accepting leads them to new life. They are different as a result of the experience.

Even those of us who are not married have probably experienced this. A friend we have known for years suddenly appears different. What is the reason? It is his new girlfriend! Somehow his new girlfriend has been able to draw out of our friend some virtues and qualities that did not appear to exist before he met her. Our friend is living a new life, and it is marvelous for him, his girlfriend, and for us. Things have changed for the better.

Again, our experience confirms what the pope says with respect to Original Unity. We can recall times when someone hurt us. It was an unpleasant experience. On the other hand, we can recall times in our lives when we felt accepted by another person. These times of acceptance are perhaps the happiest of our lives. So, too, are those times when we really give ourselves to other people. We willingly and lovingly sacrifice our own pleasure for the sake of others, and we experience a deep sense of satisfaction. This all forms part of the experience of Original Unity.

Original Nakedness

The third experience is Original Nakedness. Where and when have we ever experienced Original Nakedness? Perhaps we may recall an experience of *nudity*, such as running around the house naked as a young child. Original Nakedness, however, is more than this; it is a symbol of freedom in communication. Clearly, Original Nakedness was essential for the perfection of Original Unity. For love to be real, it must be freely given and freely accepted. So Adam and Eve were free—free from inner and outer restrictions. In other words, Adam and Eve experienced no barriers or difficulties in their communication and life together. This may seem a little odd, but remember we are examining the original experiences. God did not create barriers to communication or difficulties for people who are trying to form friendships. Those barriers come from another source—Original Sin.

> God did not create barriers to communication or difficulties for people who are trying to form friendships. Those barriers come from another source—Original Sin.

To better understand what John Paul II means by Original Nakedness, we might consider what the Book of Genesis says of Adam and Eve: they "were both naked, and were not ashamed." They were totally free. They had no inhibitions about their own bodies or the body of the other. As with the child running around naked, young children have this experience in some way. They exhibit a degree of freedom (not shame) about their bodies. They are comfortable with who they are and who other children are. The key is the fact that they are children. They have almost unlimited trust in those around them and, of course, they have not yet reached the age of reason.

So the experience of Original Nakedness goes hand in hand with freedom, which is a reality we have doubtlessly experienced. This experience is particularly strong when we decide not to "follow the crowd" (which would be a lack of freedom), choosing instead to follow the right course of action. This is the ultimate meaning of freedom. Often we become confused about the meaning of freedom. We can think that freedom is simply "making choices." But as one eminent biblical scholar, Fr. Francis Martin, has said, "Choice is a symptom of freedom." That is, we can choose because we are free.

Yet freedom is deeper than mere choice. The essence of freedom is not in making multiple choices. We are not free just because we can cram our days with one thousand and one choices. Often at the end of days like that, we feel utterly exhausted and totally unfulfilled. Freedom means deciding to surrender to the love of another. Thus it means choosing to be a better person by accepting this love and the choices that go with it. Freedom is about maturity. It is about the type of person each one of us would like to become.

For instance, if a person steals, then that person becomes a thief. A thief chooses, through freedom, not only to steal something, but also chooses to become a thief. Or take the person who decides to do his or her work well each day. By using freedom in this way, by working at his or her tasks as best he or she can, that person has become a good worker, a better human person. That person is realizing his or her freedom. This is what we mean by perfection.

St. Irenaeus, who was Bishop of Lyon in France and who died around A.D. 202, once said, "The glory of God is man fully alive." So as we use our freedom and become more and more human, we give glory to God. God, therefore, has no desire to crush us. He has no desire to inhibit our freedom. Rather, God wants the best for us. He wants us to develop our talents and, in doing so, honor him. In this sense we can see how sin is an offense against God. We offend God by offending ourselves, that is, by doing things that go against our humanity.

It is important for us to be convinced that freedom means more than choice. Yes, we do make choices, and they are important. However, freedom is more than this. It is about our willingness to let go of our lives. Through choice we can control things to such an extent that we are not free persons, but slaves. We can become "control freaks."

This is hardly freedom, but illusion. Emphasis on individual choice—on what "I want to do" with "my life"—can suffocate our freedom. Rather, freedom aims at letting go. It aims at surrendering ourselves to others so we find real maturity. And this maturity itself breeds freedom. St. Paul talks about this kind of freedom and maturity in his Letter to the Ephesians. He writes to those who are married: "Be subject to one another out of reverence for Christ. Wives, be subject to your husbands.... Husbands, love your wives, as Christ loved the church and gave himself up for her" (5:21–22, 25). John Paul II calls this "mutual subordination in Christ." Both husband and wife use their freedom to submit themselves to each other in Christ. They surrender their lives to each other, and in doing so they become free, mature human beings. They surrender their lives out of love. This is the critical point. Freedom finds its fullest expression and meaning when we make of ourselves a gift for others.

> Freedom finds its fullest expression and meaning when we make of ourselves a gift for others.

And this will entail, on more occasions than not, doing things that go against our personal desires. In this way we accept others and give ourselves to others and thus reach true human maturity and freedom.

Connected to Original Nakedness is the concept of "sexual shame." Pope John Paul II has a very positive spin on sexual shame. He says now sexual shame is good for us because it protects our purity and chastity. Originally sexual shame was not part of the plan. We were naked before each other and not ashamed. Enter Original Sin, and enter sexual shame.

Author and cultural commentator Roger Scruton notes that there is such a thing as *moral shame* and such a thing as *sexual shame*. The two are not unrelated, but should be distinguished. When we do something wrong and someone discovers our wrongdoing, we are ashamed. We might call this moral shame. Moral shame is founded on our wrongdoing and the fact that someone is judging us. But sexual shame is a little different. To be sure, if we perform a sexual act that is contrary to what we know to be right, then we may experience moral shame. Sexual shame, instead, is a "shield emotion" that protects us from abuse. Scruton says very insightfully that sexual shame arises "from the thought that we are being judged as a body, a mechanism, an *object*." Thus sexual shame is like a shield "that protects us from abuse, whether by another or ourselves." In this way, the initial negative experience of sexual shame actually turns out to be a safeguard for us. Because of sexual shame we become reluctant to perform or enter into those things we know to be sexually wrong. Shame becomes a protector and guardian of our bodily and sexual life.

Review of the Positive Original Experiences

Before we briefly consider the last original experience, we should stop here and consider what has been going on in this new approach developed by Pope John Paul II. We have not begun our reflections on the human person and the human body with a discussion about sin, but with an examination of God's original intention: his magnificent vision for us. John Paul II starts at what the Bible calls "the beginning." He starts here because this is where Christ started with the disciples. This starting point is not sinful humanity and a sinful world; rather, it is the exciting vision God has for us.

Before John Paul's teaching, we Christians knew only of Original Sin. We did not know of Original Solitude, Unity, or Nakedness. True, we might have intuited these positive experiences and had an experience of them ourselves, but we could not have named them, studied them, or articulated them for ourselves or others. They were not part and parcel of our Christian learning.

The three original experiences prior to Original Sin are present in the Bible. But they have remained latent and dormant. With John Paul II's *Theology of the Body*, these three experiences now see the light of day. They have been brought into the open for all of us to see. Pope John Paul II has done this by means of a fresh reading of the Bible in which he combines Scripture with human experience.

Original Sin remains a valid experience. Personal sin, too, is a reality in our lives. We all need to be converted from it. But what are we going to be converted to? The *Theology of the Body* suggests that we should be converted to Original Solitude, Original Unity, and Original Nakedness. We are to be converted to what God wants for us: happiness and freedom in our relationships—with him and with others. The revelation that there are three experiences prior to Original Sin, therefore, informs us of the real meaning of life. What's more, conversion of heart will be made easier, since we can see that it will be good for us as human beings. John Paul II is taking us back to our proper roots. It is only from a proper foundation that we can build anything of worth. To go back to "the beginning"—to Original Solitude, Unity, and Nakedness—means to understand that only by opening ourselves up to God, his creation, and other human beings can we mature.

> To go back to "the beginning" means to understand that only by opening ourselves up to God, his creation, and other human beings can we mature.

So now when you are asked to complete the phrase "Original _____," you will say Original Solitude, followed by Original Unity, and then Original Nakedness. Then, and only then, will you say Original Sin. This truly is a "revolution," or "time bomb."

Original Sin

Finally we arrive at Original Sin, an act of mistrust and pride (cf. Gen 3:1–19). As a result of Adam's sin, we find it hard to make the right choices. We find evil attractive. This is called concupiscence. It is like a wound in the leg; we can still walk, but only with some difficulty. We struggle to avoid bad things, and we often find it difficult to pursue good things. This is part of our human experience, too. As we can see in the three original experiences explained earlier, God had intended us to be always happy and free. Things worked out differently. We now find ourselves in a world that is still fundamentally good, but less than God wanted. So we encounter people who are basically good, but who have sins, faults, and weaknesses.

We encounter ourselves, too, and here the story is the same. We are basically good, but we give in to temptation and sin. St. Paul describes this reality marvelously in the Bible in chapter seven of his Letter to the Romans. Find some time to read it, but then read chapter eight, which talks of life in the Spirit. It is good to know that one of the greatest theologians and saints found the going tough, too.

Original Sin and concupiscence affect the other original experiences. We find it hard to sense God in our lives. Some people express severe doubts, even disbelief, in God. They are called agnostics or atheists. The experience of Original Solitude is not automatic, but requires some effort. So does the experience of Original Unity. People find it hard to get along with each other and to accept each other for who they are. In addition, people find it hard to be generous and to give of themselves. Likewise, sin takes away our experience of freedom—Original Nakedness. We find it easier to do bad things and harder to do good things.

But we have the Gospel. We have Jesus Christ, who saved us and redeemed us from these difficulties. Jesus Christ—true God and true man—has reestablished the meaning of human existence. He has restored and redeemed those original experiences. How has he done this? By offering his body on the cross as an act of love for us.

With this positive note, let us go to chapter two and examine the four qualities of the human body, which are developed from the four original human experiences. In a sense, the four original experiences are our means to understand God's view of the body.

Chapter Two

The Four Qualities
of the Human Body

Chapter one introduced and explained the four original experiences. To review briefly: until the teaching of Pope John Paul II, Christians had been familiar with only one original experience: Original Sin. That is something we can all name; it is part of our vocabulary. But John Paul II wants to take us back to "the beginning," as Christ took his disciples back to "the beginning." He wants to take us back before Original Sin formed part of our experience.

What do we find at "the beginning"? What does the Book of Genesis reveal to us? Aided by reference to human experience, Pope John Paul's *Theology of the Body* reveals three original experiences *prior* to Original Sin. That was the import of chapter one. We have discovered the revolution of thought John Paul II has bequeathed to the Church. We have detonated a "theological time bomb."

We have discovered and have begun to understand the meaning of Original Solitude, Original Unity, and Original Nakedness. In examining these three original experiences, we gain insight into the nature of the human body, the human person, and human relationships. Just as we made discoveries about the original experiences in chapter one, so in chapter two we are about to make some very significant discoveries about the human body.

As we make our way through chapter two, it will be worthwhile remembering that we can make these new discoveries about the human body because we are able to enter into the original experiences. This point was made clear in the previous chapter: John Paul II wants each of us to have an experience of solitude, of unity, and of nakedness. When we allow ourselves to have these experiences, then we begin to understand more fully the meaning of life, the human body, and human relationships.

The *Theology of the Body* is a sophisticated and systematic body of thought. There can be no doubt about that. However, we do not have to be rocket scientists to understand the *Theology of the Body*. We need no special training or higher degrees. Rather, we will come to understand the *Theology of the Body* by letting ourselves enter into the original experiences. In other words, if we let ourselves *live* Original Solitude, Unity, and Nakedness, then we will come to understand how the human body is *symbolic, nuptial,* and *free*.

Now let's outline the connection between the original experiences discussed in chapter one and the qualities of the human body that we will discover and understand here in chapter two.

1. From the experience of Original Solitude, we understand that the human body is *symbolic*.

2. From the experience of Original Unity, we come to realize that the human body is *nuptial*.

3. From the experiences of Original Nakedness and Original Sin, we realize that the human body is *free* and *fallen*.

4. From the experience of knowing and loving Jesus Christ, we come to understand that the human body is *redeemed*.

Chapter two will examine each of these points, with points one and four receiving the most attention. Most of us will not be familiar with the first point, which is that the human body is symbolic. We need to examine this idea thoroughly, and when we do we will understand the next point, which is that the human body is nuptial. A little time will be spent on point three, the body is free and fallen, and then I will devote a substantial section of the chapter to point four, the human body is redeemed.

Before delving into these four points, consider how Christ takes us back to "the beginning." He wants to open up for us God's intention and desire for us by granting us the experiences of Original Solitude, Unity, and Nakedness. These experiences, however, have become more elusive because of Original Sin. Christ comes to restore and renew the original experiences. He comes to take us back to "the beginning."

But how does he do this? This question can only be answered by asking these questions: who is Christ, and what does he do? And furthermore, how do we have access to him in the twenty-first century? Can he be made real? Can we really experience him as a living person, or is he simply a figure of the past? I attempt to address these critical questions in the latter part of this chapter. Now let's try to discover what Pope John Paul II means when he says the human body is symbolic.

The Human Body Is Symbolic

Recall the experience of Original Solitude. It had a positive and a negative dimension. Positively, Adam realized that he was different from the rest of creation. Adam sensed that he was superior to the created world, even though he formed part of it. Negatively, Adam could not find another body like his. He was alone. Both these dimensions make up the experience of Original Solitude.

Adam realized that he had a special connection with God. True, we are like the rest of creation in that we are made of matter. Like the animals, we have bodies. But our bodies are different, and thus there is more to us than our bodies. In other words, there is more to us than meets the eye.

We have an invisible dimension. We can think in a way animals can't, and we can reach up to God, our Creator, to communicate with him as the animals can't. We can know and love. We can relate to God intimately. Furthermore, human beings can relate intimately with each other. We are, therefore, a mixture—a unity—of what is seen and what is unseen. We have a visible and an invisible dimension, which is why we were given that special responsibility of naming the animals.

But these two dimensions—the visible and invisible—are not separate. They have been, in a sense, thrown together. This is precisely what we mean by the word *symbol*. The word is derived from a Greek word that means *to be thrown together*. In the case of human beings, the visible and the invisible are thrown together. Both are real, and both make up the human person.

So when we speak of the human body as being symbolic, we mean that the human body is more than just matter. It is also the bearer of the invisible. A symbol *makes present* something that is invisible. A symbol is something seen that immediately points our attention to something unseen, but real. A symbol, therefore, connects, or unites, the visible world and the invisible world. A symbol is perfectly natural and thus is not artificial.

Therefore, when we say the human body is symbolic, we mean that the human body has this capacity to point beyond itself. Sure enough, the body can be seen, and these physical, material dimensions have a meaning. Doctors, scientists, naturopaths, etc., all study these important physical and material dimensions.

> The human body points beyond itself to the spiritual and invisible dimensions of the human person.

But the human body points beyond itself to the spiritual and invisible dimensions of the human person. So when we think of a friend, we think not only of what he or she looks like—his or her body. We also think of the person's personality, character, ability to think, etc. In other words, we think of the person's invisible or spiritual reality.

We call the innermost aspect of a human person the soul. It is our spiritual principle. It is our source of unity. Animals have souls, too, but their souls are material. Human beings, instead, have spiritual souls. To say that the human body is symbolic is to say there is a depth to a human person that is not visible. In this, we are different from the animals.

Ponder this carefully. We human beings live in a world of symbols. Animals live in the real world, but they do not live in a world of symbols. Animals have bodies, but unlike us they do not have spiritual souls. True, animals do respond to signs. A dog, for instance, can be taught to respond to a particular hand signal. A horse will jump at the prompting of its rider. In addition, animals can be exceedingly loyal to their human master. They seem to possess affection and feelings we would normally think of as reserved for human beings. They do, therefore, possess an invisible dimension, but it is fair to say that their invisible world is not the human world of symbol, but more the world of sign.

Human beings are both visible and invisible, and we bring these two worlds together in our thinking, actions, and language—in our lives. As William May, a prominent moral theologian, expresses it, human beings are *body-persons*. The body is in time and space; the spirit is in eternity. We live in both worlds. This is unique to us as human beings.

For instance, a teacher, after explaining a topic to her class, notices that one of the students looks confused. She says to the student, "Melissa, don't you see what I am trying to say?" Seeing is a physical act. Yet the teacher uses it to designate understanding. Seeing is symbolic for comprehension and insight. When we speak of the world of symbol, we are thinking about this deep connection between the physical and spiritual world. It is natural to us. We live in this symbolic world each day, but we very rarely think or reflect about it, and thus we are unaware of it. In a sense we take it for granted.

Consider the five senses. All of them have a physical and spiritual meaning. The sense of *touch* is critical for carrying on our daily lives. Driving a car would be impossible without it. But notice the role it plays in communicating love. People who love each other touch each other. Mothers cuddle their children. Husbands and wives caress each other. Touch is symbolic of love. When a person touches another, he or she transmits love—something that is invisible, but real. Human touch transmits affection.

The sense of *hearing* is related to attentiveness and interest in what a person has to say. Again, it is a symbol of love. *Seeing* is related to understanding, to comprehending intellectually. In fact, in his Gospel St. John equates seeing with believing. When you believe in Jesus Christ, you see life in a new way.

Smell is related to curiosity. Someone is said to be "nosy" when they get involved in matters that don't concern them. *Taste* is related to hunger and thirst, and thus spiritual desire. Psalm 63 says: "O God, you are my God, for you I long; for you my soul is thirsting. My body pines for you like a dry, weary land without water."

I am sure you get the idea. Just read the newspaper each day, and you will see literally hundreds of examples of the world of symbol. There you will read of "dark clouds brewing on the horizon" for some company experiencing financial difficulties, and of a newly aroused "hunger for thriller novels." The list is almost endless.

This is the world of symbol in which we live, and it is confirmed by the second negative dimension of Original Solitude. Adam could not find another body like his. There were plenty of bodily creatures out there in God's creation, but none of them had a body like his. He could not form a partnership with any of them.

But he could with Eve. This difference was another way Adam experienced the symbolic nature of the human body. Only Eve's body was symbolic; the animal bodies were bodies, but not symbolic. Unlike animal bodies, which simply make present the animal body and its instincts, the human body *makes present* the whole person, visible and invisible.

The Human Body Is Nuptial

As soon as Adam saw Eve, he knew something was different. Here was another human body, which he could relate to intimately. Eve was complementary to him. This meant that they could be one. Think a minute about the intimate details of a man and woman. Men and women look different. A man's body is stronger, more muscular, and tougher. A woman's body is more supple and delicate. Touch a man's body and compare it with a woman's body; it is different.

Think, too, of the sexual differences. The man's genitals are external, while the woman's are internal. They are made for each other. The man enters the woman in sexual intercourse, and the woman receives him. They become "one flesh."

When John Paul II says the human body is nuptial, he means that the human body is meant for love—it is made for relationship. You can see how this flows from the symbolic nature of the human body. A man and woman find each other attractive. They not only experience a physical attraction, but also a spiritual attraction. They marry and they come together sexually.

This act is both physical and spiritual since the body is symbolic. Therefore, when a man and woman come together, they do so as symbolic creatures. They touch each other, they speak words of love, and through these actions and words they communicate love to each other. Sex is, therefore, a profoundly mysterious and beautiful act. It is not a "casual indoor sport."

Because the human body is symbolic and nuptial, when a man and woman make love in sexual intercourse, they are communicating. In other words, the human body has a language, and so does sex. Pope John Paul II says sex is a unique form of language. *Sex is body language*.

Seriously consider how the human body is symbolic. The body speaks. The human body says: "Look, this body is real—you can see it. It is made of matter. It is clearly visible to others." It is, however, a body different from animal bodies. So in addition to saying that it is visible, the human body says: "This body of mine points beyond itself. This body of mine points you to my deeper self—my heart (will), intellect, and memory. My body makes present the whole of my person. My body is a symbolic body—a visible reality that carries my inner reality."

Seriously consider, too, how the human body is nuptial. The human body says: "Look, this body is made for love—for an abiding relationship. My body is not made for just sensual pleasure, because there is more to me than just the sensual. My body is symbolic, and all that I do has an extraordinary spiritual dimension. I express my love—my profound spiritual reality—in and through my body."

The human body speaks; it has a language of its own. Therefore, sex, a bodily activity, has a language. Sex speaks a language of sensual pleasure; there can be no doubt about this. But it also speaks a spiritual language, a language of love. By touching each other, listening to each other, looking at each other, and entering and receiving each other, a man and woman communicate in the most intimate way. They communicate sensually and spiritually. They communicate as body-persons. Sex speaks forcefully of love.

> By touching each other, listening to each other, looking at each other, and entering and receiving each other, a man and woman communicate in the most intimate way.

In the next chapter, we will examine closely the issue of contraception. But we can, I think, begin to see what is wrong with it. Contraception contradicts the language of love, the language of the body. It alters the language of love. In his pastoral letter *Marriage: A Communion of Life and Love*, Bishop Victor Galeon, of the Diocese of St. Augustine, Florida, writes:

God designed married love to be expressed in a special language—the body language of the sexual act. In fact, sexual communication uses many of the same terms that verbal communication does: intercourse, to know (carnally), to conceive, etc. With this in mind, let's pose some questions: Is it normal for a wife to insert earplugs while listening to her husband? Is it normal for a husband to muffle his mouth while speaking to his wife? These examples are so abnormal as to appear absurd. Yet if such behavior is abnormal for verbal communication, why do we tolerate a wife using a diaphragm or the pill, or a husband employing a condom during sexual communication?

Contraception, then, like other sexual aberrations, contradicts, alters, and ultimately destroys the symbolic and nuptial meaning of the human body. We will see this more clearly in chapter three.

The Human Body Is Free and Fallen

Before Original Sin the human body, and thus the human person, was free. We saw this in chapter one. The third original experience is called Original Nakedness, and it is symbolic of freedom in communication. We saw, too, that in order to love, the human person must be free, and this is exactly what Original Nakedness means. How can we say the human body and the human person are meant for love unless they are fundamentally free? Freedom is a necessary condition for love. Without freedom, a man and woman could not give or accept love.

However, the body of the human person is affected by Original Sin. We noted the effects of Original Sin in chapter one. The human body is not the cause of sin. Sin belongs to our spiritual nature, but because we are a unity of body and soul—because we live symbolically—sin affects the human body. In fact, we will all experience the fallen nature of the human body in a radical way when we die. Death is a consequence of Original Sin.

Think about death for a minute. Why would God create us to die? That doesn't make sense. God is a God of life. He desires that we have life and have it to the fullest. As the Bible's Book of Wisdom says, "God did not make death, and he does not delight in the death of the living. For he created all things that they might exist" (1:13–14) So death has its origin somewhere else, and according to Christian teaching, death is one of the consequences of Original Sin.

Besides death, one of the other consequences of Original Sin is disordered sexual desire. For example, a man can lust after a woman (or vice versa). He can come to see her only as a sexual object, something to be used for a short time of pleasure and then discarded. He can begin to look at a woman only in terms of her physical attributes and forget her invisible dimension. In other words, sin can make it hard to see how the human body is symbolic. We see a lot of evidence of this nowadays. Television, magazines, and the Web often carry images—particularly of women—that highlight only the physical dimension of the human body. They fail to tell us the real truth of the human person.

The Human Body Is Redeemed

But all is not lost. Christ, through his death and resurrection, restores to each one of us the meaning of human existence and the human body. His body was crucified. His bodily death is the cause of our bodily renewal. The soldier pierced his body and out flowed blood and water, the "fountain of sacramental life in the Church" (The Roman Missal). Then after his resurrection Jesus appeared to his disciples and let them touch his body. Thomas put his finger into the side of Jesus. He believed because of this bodily experience.

In fact, after the death and resurrection of Jesus Christ, our lives are even better than before Original Sin. God has now entered history. The Father has sent his Son. God, who is entirely beyond our sight, is now visible to us. In addition, because God has been made flesh, he can now be touched, tasted, smelled, and heard. This is incredible, to say the least!

God has entered history and in the person of Jesus Christ is now our most faithful friend. St. Teresa of Avila, who lived in the sixteenth century, reflected deeply on the friendship of Christ. She wrote:

> Christ gives us help and strength, never deserts us, and is true and sincere in his friendship.... What more do we want than to have at our side a friend so loyal that he will never desert us when we are in trouble or in difficulties, as worldly friends do? How blessed is the person who genuinely and sincerely loves Jesus and holds on to him! (from the Divine Office for the feast of St. Teresa of Avila)

In other words, Christ is now ours. He is the most intimate of friends, far more faithful and intimate than anyone we can imagine. Because of this we can know him, relate to him, and love him. This is the great bonus that has come to us: our sin is wiped out, our lives have been restored, and we have been raised to a new life with Christ.

> Christ is now ours. He is the most intimate of friends, far more faithful and intimate than anyone we can imagine.

Christ Takes Us Back to "the Beginning"

Let us pause here for a moment and learn more about Jesus. Who is he? What is Jesus' real identity? What does he do? How does he take us back to "the beginning"? The apostle John answers this question in the opening line of his Gospel. "In the beginning was the Word, and the Word was with God, and the Word was God."

Jesus is the *Word*. What do we mean when we say Jesus is the Word? What is a word? We could give lots of definitions of a word, but its deepest meaning lies in the fact that a word is *from someone* and spoken *to someone*. A word is *from* and *to*.

Stop and think about this deeply. A word is a very *intimate* reality. A word comes from the inmost part of one person and is spoken to the inmost part of another person. This is especially true of words of love, truth, and hope. But because words are so common, we can lose sight of this. Words can become cheap. With the mass media, words can become almost meaningless. In addition, people often use very harmful words; words can be used to deceive. Because of this it becomes difficult to see the beauty of a word and the deepest reality of what a word is.

But in itself, a word is beautiful. At their deepest level words establish, sustain, and perfect human relationships. They come from within one person and reach the heart of another person. A word literally enters a person. A word, therefore, is a gift one person gives to another.

Once again, check out your own experience. Haven't you at times listened to someone speak from the heart? At these times you can recognize with clarity that a word is "from someone to someone." A word is from heart to heart, and as a consequence a word can change your life.

Could there be anything, then, more intimate and gracious than a word? What if a word were actually a person? What if there could be a person solely from someone and solely for someone? Yes, this would be remarkable. This would be a *word-person*.

Well, Jesus is this person. He is the Word spoken by the Father to us. God has spoken clearly and definitively. He has spoken with so much clarity and force that this Word cannot only be heard, as with other words, but this Word can be touched, seen, and tasted! This Word has become flesh.

To say that Jesus is the Word is to say that he is from the Father—that *he is God*. To say that Jesus is the Word made flesh is to say that he is now in the flesh— that *he is man*. Jesus is truly God and truly human. He is the God-man who is from the Father, given as gift for us. He is the Word spoken to us.

> Christ and the events of his life belong to our time now. They are eternally present, and the word of God makes them present.

As Word, Jesus speaks to us in two ways. He speaks in the same way we speak. He carries on conversations with people, and we have access to these dialogues in the four Gospels. Because he is a prophet, he teaches us. His teaching, too, can be found in the Gospels. Through his words and teaching, Jesus takes us back to "the beginning." This is the first way Christ speaks to us.

But Jesus also speaks to us with his life and activities. He was born of the Virgin Mary and had to learn how to talk, walk, work, rest, socialize, etc. His parents taught him how to pray. He lived in a small village for most of his life, working, it seems, as a carpenter. All of this speaks to us of the importance of our ordinary daily life. God enters daily life, lives in it, loves it, and makes it his own.

At the age of thirty, when according to Jewish custom rabbis began their function as teachers, Jesus entered public life and began a ministry of teaching, healing, forgiving sins, and raising people from the dead. He had such an impact that the authorities put him to death as a common criminal. He died on a cross, but three days later he rose from the dead.

Christ's death and resurrection is his final and supreme work. On the cross, Jesus offered his life to his Father, and he did this for our salvation. Jesus literally died for us. God the Father accepted this offering and raised him from the dead on the third day. By this act, we have received forgiveness for our sins, and we have been granted a new life with Christ.

This new life with Christ is given to us as a gift in two specific ways. We *receive* the word of God. During his time on earth, Jesus *said* and *did* things. These realities are contained in the Gospels of Matthew, Mark, Luke, and John. When we read the word of God, however, we are not just reading a historical book. Rather, we are being brought into living contact with Jesus Christ.

For instance, when Pope John Paul II went to the Holy Land in the year 2000, he celebrated Mass in the city of Bethlehem, where Jesus was born. In his homily, the pope quoted St. Bede, who lived in the eighth century: "Still today, and every day until the end of the ages, the Lord will be continually conceived in Nazareth and born in Bethlehem." Christ and the events of his life belong to history, but they also belong to our time now. They are eternally present, and the word of God *makes them present*. We really meet and receive Christ when we encounter him in his word. Theology has a technical name for this reality. It says that the word of God *mediates* Christ and his life. In this way, we receive Christ into our lives, and he receives us into his. Christ, then, is our contemporary. We can know him and love him.

In addition, we receive Christ in the sacraments. We die and rise with Christ in Baptism. We live a new life with him—a life dead to sin and alive to Christ. In the Holy Eucharist, we are present at Christ's death, resurrection, and ascension. This is made possible by the consecration of bread into Christ's body and the consecration of wine into Christ's blood. Then we are given the opportunity to receive Christ's body and blood. We do not receive only a sign or an image, but we really receive Christ. We receive him, he receives us, and our wounds are healed. In the sacrament of Reconciliation, we are forgiven our sins, just as Jesus forgave the sinners who came to him seeking mercy.

So we have total, free, and spontaneous access to Christ in the twenty-first century. Time is no barrier.

This means, too, that Christ is able to restore the original experiences we discovered in chapter one, and it means that he is able to restore the meaning of the human body we have encountered here in chapter two. Christ is able to take us back to "the beginning," and this allows us to see the full meaning of our lives.

Before we move to chapter three, let's be clear on what we have discovered so far. By referring to the word of God and human experience, Pope John Paul II has developed four original experiences. Three of these experiences (Original Solitude, Original Unity, and Original Nakedness) are prior to Original Sin. This is the "theological time bomb." Before the *Theology of the Body*, we were not familiar with any original experiences except sin. But John Paul II shows us how Christ takes us back to "the beginning" and in doing so projects us into the future. We can see human life, our relationships, and our lives in a totally new and positive perspective. We have discovered a gem.

From these three new original experiences and from the experience of Original Sin, we can understand that our human body is symbolic, nuptial, free, fallen, and redeemed. The body makes present the entire person. We are symbolic creatures, and because this is so, our bodies—we ourselves—are meant for love. Our bodies are not meant for lust, but for love. Thus we have discovered, in a profound sense, that our bodies are more relational than they are sexual. This helps us see that sex is important precisely because relationships are important. Our bodies, too, are free but wounded.

Finally, in and through Christ Jesus we come to a deep awareness that our bodies, and thus our very selves, are redeemed. Our experience of knowing and loving Christ helps us enter into the original experiences and thus come to a deeper understanding of who we are and what our lives can be. Let's now move to chapter three and see what the *Theology of the Body* has to say with respect to specific sexual issues.

Chapter Three

The *Theology of the Body* and Sexual Activity

Sex is an important part of our lives. We of all people know this, living as we are in a *sexually saturated society*. Sex has been elevated to a new level of consciousness. We are told that even cars are sexy! Sex has been used to serve selfish, pleasure-seeking activity. John Paul II has responded marvelously to this new scenario. He has placed sexuality within the wider context of the *Theology of the Body*. In chapters one and two we have seen what this means. Only in the light of the original human experiences and the qualities of the human body can we hope to understand the meaning and value of sexuality and sexual acts. Ripped from its proper context of healthy, stable, and committed relationships, sex becomes a mere toy.

This chapter will examine some sexual acts and view them in light of the *Theology of the Body*. Before we do that, however, we shall look briefly at the prevailing historical and cultural situation with respect to marriage during Christ's lifetime. Paradoxically, divorce was common and marriage rates were low when Christ lived. Christ delivered his teaching on marriage and divorce, therefore, at a time similar to our own in some respects.

It is important to realize that Christ taught the truth about marriage at a time when marriage was not held in high esteem. But he taught it nevertheless. The Church in our own times is called to do the same.

After a brief look at the historical and cultural situation at the time of Christ, I will briefly outline the Church's teaching on marriage as a covenant. This is important since the Church derives her sexual teaching from her understanding of marriage. In chapter one we discovered three new original experiences, and in chapter two we recognized that the human body is symbolic, nuptial, and free. When these elements are brought together, they form a unity that we call the covenant of marriage. We need to spend some time, then, discussing the covenant of marriage, and from this foundation we will be able to understand the value and morality of various sexual acts. We shall examine premarital sex, contraception, natural family planning, pornography, masturbation, oral sex, and homosexual acts.

Christ Takes Marriage Back to "the Beginning"

During the time of Jesus, two things were happening with regard to marriage. On the one hand, divorce was permissible and common among the Jewish people. We know this from the question the Pharisees put to Jesus. Moses had allowed divorce. Jesus said it had been allowed because of the people's hardness of heart. Christ called the people back to a deeper understanding of marriage in which divorce would not be an option.

On the other hand, Christ lived in a land occupied by a foreign power. Roman society had low marriage rates. The situation was so bad that on several occasions Roman emperors decreed men should marry. Marriage rates were low, it seems, because men preferred to do their own thing and live a single, carefree life. The decrees, however, had little effect. Marriage rates continued to decline.

Within this context, Jesus took his audience back to "the beginning." Jesus reaffirmed the truth of marriage even though marriage rates were low and divorce rates were high. Taking his cue from Christ, Pope John Paul II developed his *Theology of the Body* by himself going back to "the beginning" in order to develop and articulate three original experiences prior to Original Sin, which have helped us to recognize some key qualities of the human body. Now we need to see the way these original experiences and qualities of the human body contribute to our understanding of how marriage is a covenant.

The Covenant of Marriage and Divorce

A covenant is an agreement or a bond freely established between two parties. The Old Testament is all about God's covenant with his people. Noah was the first to receive it, then Abraham in spectacular fashion, and then Moses. You can read about these events in the Bible's books of Genesis and Exodus. The covenant is a contract written in blood. The parties exchange not *things*, but *themselves*. Even now, this is what God does in his covenant with us. He gives us his very life, and in return we are asked to give our lives to him.

Recall the words of the Book of Genesis. On seeing the woman, the man undertakes a radical change in his life. He clings to his wife. Furthermore, we are told the man and woman come together and form one flesh. In other words, they form a covenant. They accept each other and give themselves to each other. They give not something, but everything. They give their whole persons.

In doing this, husband and wife establish an *indissoluble bond*. Marriage is not like an aspirin tablet that can be dissolved. Rather, marriage is a rock strong enough to withstand the chaotic weather patterns of life. It is a covenant.

The covenant God establishes with his people has two critical aspects. On the one hand, the people *participate* in the covenant. In the Old Testament, this is done in a variety of ways: sacrifice is offered, a male is circumcised, a man and woman marry, etc. In the New Testament, the New Covenant is established in the definitive form of Christ's death on the cross. We celebrate this covenant in the Eucharist, in which participation is totally real and active. Christ hands over his body and blood under the form of bread and wine to be consumed with faith by us.

> Marriage is a rock strong enough to withstand the chaotic weather patterns of life. It is a covenant.

On the other hand, the people themselves *make present* the covenant by the way they live. When God gave Moses the Ten Commandments on Mount Sinai, God told him if the people kept the commandments faithfully, they would be free. In other words, they would be just like God. And by their freedom, the people of Israel would be a living sign of God himself to other people. They would be witnesses. God would be made present on earth by the way people lived.

Marriage does just this. As a sacrament, it *participates* in the New Covenant established by Christ, and, in addition, marriage *makes present* the self-giving love of this New Covenant. When a man and woman marry, they receive the sacramental blessings of the New Covenant. God lets them share in his faithful love; they participate in the covenant.

To further illustrate, recall what happened to Adam in the Garden. When Adam realized that he could not find another body like his own, God put him to sleep. The word translated as "sleep" indicates that God is performing a highly mysterious and significant divine activity. When Adam awakes from this sleep—from God's mysterious activity—something remarkable happens. God himself takes Adam and shows him the woman. God takes the initiative first. Then, and only then, does Adam act. God is creating marriage and establishing it as a covenant. In a way, marriage is like a newborn baby. It is created from nothing and can never be destroyed. Marriage is an act of God's creation. It is a gift.

But the faithful love between husband and wife is also like a *mirror*. By looking into the mirror that is marriage—by experiencing the faithful love between husband and wife—we come to know the faithful love of God. Marriage *makes present* God's faithfulness, God's covenant.

Every man and every woman is created in the image and likeness of God. Because of this, they can participate in God's very life and make God present on earth. However, God desires more. He desires that man and woman become one and so become an even stronger, clearer image of God.

God himself said it was not good for the man to be alone. God desires unity and community, not that we should live as isolated individuals. We are not called to be islands. Rather, he desires that we live in unity and friendship, since he himself is a profound unity of love in the Trinity: Father, Son, and Spirit. Made in his image, we are called to live as he does.

> When a man and woman come together in marriage, they become a much clearer and more robust image of God.

Hence, when a man and woman come together in marriage, they become a much clearer and more robust image of God. John Paul II teaches that "man becomes the image of God, not so much in the moment of solitude as in the *moment of communion*." What does this mean?

We sense God in a number of ways; for example, we can sense him in nature. We experience the beauty of creation, and we come to realize, in an imperfect way, that God really exists. He has left traces of himself behind in his work of creation. Furthermore, we experience ourselves as unique, and we experience other human beings as unique. These experiences lead us to God.

But when we experience and witness the love between a man and woman, we gain a much deeper insight into God. The *experience of love* is compelling. We begin to realize, as the Gospel of John says, that God is love. The love between a man and woman is the greatest sign we have that God is real, that God exists. Marriage, therefore, is the greatest image we have of God.

This is what John Paul II means when he says that man becomes the image of God not so much in solitude as in communion. Adam was alone in the Garden. Made in the image and likeness of God, he reflected and mirrored God. He could act like God. He could participate in God's life. Nevertheless, he was alone. Something was missing. Eve joined him, and together as a "one-flesh" union they made God present in a way neither of them could have done alone. God is made present more by communion than by solitude. We become the image of God not so much in solitude as in communion.

Marriage is thus a covenant that both participates in God's very life and makes him present on earth. A marriage is established in the exact same way as the Book of Genesis describes. Two acts are needed. First, the man and woman commit to each other for life, until the death of either one. Then, by means of sexual intercourse, they consummate the marriage. Consummate means to "perfect" or to "bring to a higher level of fulfillment." Both these elements—the vows and sexual intercourse—must be present for an indissoluble bond to be established. Through these two distinct but not separate acts, a "one-flesh" union is established. The covenant of marriage is brought into existence.

Premarital Sex and Living Together

We can see that the covenant of marriage flows directly from the original human experiences and the qualities of the human body. Human beings are unique, for they are in solitude with God and have bodies that are symbolic. Furthermore, the experience of solitude leads to the experience of unity. Human beings are made for love. Their bodies are nuptial, and this is why a man and woman can become "one flesh."

Sex does not belong only to the physical world. Rather, sex belongs to the world of symbol and the world of love. Sex is not a casual pastime or a mere toy, devoid of any coherent meaning. Nor can sex be reduced to an experimental activity; it is not like test-driving a car. It is not something we do to see if a relationship might work. Sex is much more than that. Sex consummates. It elevates the relationship between a man and woman, bringing it to a higher, more perfect level. Sex places on sacred ground the love a man and woman share. Sex is mysterious precisely because it is symbolic and nuptial. It therefore needs protection. It needs the words of commitment that are spoken on the wedding day.

Sex is thus the *seal* on a relationship—not the beginning of a relationship. When a man and woman enter into a sexual relationship before marriage, they can easily confuse sexual pleasure for love. They may not be *in love*, but *in lust*, and this may well be the reason why those who marry after living together have a divorce rate that is 50 percent higher than that of those who do not cohabitate before marriage.

Recent studies show that for a woman, the sexual act is tremendously significant. A woman releases *bonding hormones* three times in her life: during sexual intercourse, while giving birth, and while nursing or breast-feeding. Notice that they are called "bonding hormones." "Hormone" is a physical term, and "bonding" a spiritual term. It is a symbolic term used by medical professionals. Clearly, sexual intercourse should be accompanied by a deep and abiding commitment. This commitment is marriage.

Sex within marriage, then, leads to a profound experience of unity. On the other hand, someone who has sex with a number of people before marriage leaves part of him or herself with those other people. A part of the self is left with person A, part with person B, and so on. This divides the person within him or herself, which will make life difficult. Virginity and chastity are safeguards against this danger.

Of course, sex is not only a love act. It is also a life act. Sex has more than one meaning. A prominent writer in this area, Professor Janet Smith, recommends that when you are dating someone, you ask yourself the question, "Do I really want to have babies with this person? Do I want to be the mother or father of this person's child?" This is a good question. More likely than not, it will eliminate a lot of people whom you find sexually attractive but would not want to marry.

Contraception

The word "contraception" means "against conception." Contraception takes various forms. The man may withdraw his penis and ejaculate outside the woman's body. He may place a condom on his penis, which prevents the sperm from entering the woman. In addition, the man may have radical surgery that makes him infertile (a vasectomy). For her part, the woman may take oral contraceptives, place a variety of devices in her vagina or uterus, have radical surgery that makes her infertile (a tubal ligation), or use other methods.

Contraception is any act done either *before sex*, *during sex*, or *after sex* that is intended to prevent the conception of a new life. The Church has always taught that contraception is wrong, but it has used different reasons over time. I will give two reasons utilizing the *Theology of the Body*.

First, sex is an act that may result in a new human being coming into existence. For this to happen, God needs to create the soul of the new human being. In other words, sex is the *sacred space* of God. Sex is where God likes to work to continue his gift of creation. Remember: for a new life to come into existence, God must create a soul from nothing. The parents supply the sperm and ovum during an act of intercourse—an act of love—and God creates the soul.

Therefore, each human person is totally unique, totally unrepeatable, not only genetically, but also spiritually. All this takes place when husband and wife engage in sex. Because God creates within the setting of human love, husband and wife should not deliberately exclude God. They should not contracept. Rather, they should be open to the possibility of new life.

But doesn't God allow us to develop and use technology? Why can't we use contraceptives to regulate the conception of children? We can, after all, take an aspirin to soothe a headache. The argument is persuasive but flawed. A headache is a *curse*, while fertility is a *blessing*. Contraceptives are not at all like medications. Contraceptives prevent the blessing of a child, while medications heal a sickness.

In addition, the human body is symbolic. It is intimately related to the spiritual world. Because we are symbolic creatures, we cannot divorce the physical and spiritual world. If we do, we lose the meaning of human life. The source of both the physical and spiritual world is God. We can use technology to *enhance* this symbolic world, but never to *frustrate* or *destroy* it. That is what contraception does.

We could use contraceptives if we were mere animals. But we are not. We are sexual-symbolic beings. Notice that we say animals *reproduce*, while humans *procreate*. This is an important difference. Animals reproduce themselves, while humans do not. By engaging in sexual acts, husband and wife are open not to reproduction, but to procreation. In other words, they are opening themselves up to another adult human being who is a body-person, and they are opening themselves to God. Their sexual love may result in the creation of an entirely unique person. This is a far cry from the world of animal reproduction.

We have touched on the second reason in our reference to the world of symbol. The second reason, however, also refers to the nuptial meaning of the human body. Let us look at this more closely. We have seen that the nuptial meaning of the human body is this: the human body is meant for love. John Paul II explains clearly that upon discovering the woman, the man decides to become "one flesh" with his wife. The man accepts his wife, and he gives himself to her (and vice versa). It is a mutual act. Both of them do it freely.

> Sex is the open, honest communication between husband and wife.

In order to love his wife, the man has to accept his wife for who she is. He cannot have any significant reservation about her. He must love her unreservedly. To ask her to take a contraceptive pill, to place an IUD in her body, or to have a tubal ligation would amount to a lack of acceptance. And as we have seen, it would crush the symbolism of the human body and of sexual intercourse.

To contracept in any way is like saying: "I love you, but not all of you." This would happen, too, if a man decided to contracept with a condom. He would be saying to his wife: "I love you, but I don't want to give you that crucial part of me that is my sperm—our possible future child." Contraception is contrary, therefore, to the nuptial meaning of the human body. Through contraception, a couple use, rather than love, each other. To return to sex as the language of the body mentioned in chapter two, sex is the open, honest communication between husband and wife. To contracept is to tell a lie with one's body.

Natural Family Planning

Do husband and wife have to intend having a baby every time they have sex? No, they need only reverence the sexual act and remain open to each other and to the possibility of new life. They should simply intend to have sex in the fullness of love. They can engage in sexual love to make each other happy, heal an argument, relax, have some fun, etc. They can engage in sexual activity for its own sake. Sex is a good thing, and husband and wife don't necessarily need any added reason to do it. They can have sex because sex is good.

Does the Church specify how many children husband and wife should have? Once again the answer is no. Couples are free to decide this. If there are just reasons for spacing children (i.e., delaying the conception of a child), then husband and wife are asked to use those methods referred to as Natural Family Planning (NFP) methods.

Actually, NFP methods would be better called symbolic or nuptial methods because they respect the symbolic and nuptial meaning of the human body. In contrast to artificial methods, NFP *preserves* and enhances the experiences of Original Unity and Original Nakedness.

When husband and wife practice NFP, they give of themselves without any significant reservation, and they accept each other without any significant reservation. Original Unity is respected and lived. Recourse to artificial methods of contraception, as we have seen above, destroys this experience of unity since the husband and wife are no longer respecting the nuptial meaning of the body. Contraception leads to disunity, while NFP facilitates intimacy, unity, and love.

> When husband and wife practice NFP, they give of themselves without any significant reservation, and they accept each other without any significant reservation.

In addition, husband and wife experience Original Nakedness. This is the original experience that allows human persons to realize and discover their freedom. Recalling what was said in chapter one, we recognize that Original Nakedness is a symbol for freedom in communication. This is precisely what happens in NFP.

NFP encourages husband and wife to communicate about their sexuality and fertility. The man is fertile twenty-four hours a day, seven days a week. But his wife is fertile only for a few days during her monthly cycle. A married couple using NFP will communicate with each other. The wife will tell her husband when she is fertile and when she is not. Her husband will listen. This communication obviously strengthens their intimacy and marriage bond.

This claim is supported by recent statistics. Couples who use NFP have a divorce rate of one percent, while the average divorce rate in most Western countries is between 40 percent and 50 percent. It will be worth your while, therefore, to find out more about NFP. Simply type in "natural methods of family planning" or "natural fertility regulation" on the World Wide Web, and you will find many sources.

The Church gives *four reasons* as to when these natural methods can be used to delay conception. There may be *physical* difficulties, such as the health of one of the spouses, etc. There may be *psychological* reasons, such as when one or both of the spouses experiences anxiety or depression, etc. There may be *economic* reasons, such as various types of financial difficulties, etc. There may be *social* reasons—a war, a drought, undue family tension, etc. The reasons must be just, and this will often depend upon circumstances. Delaying children for an overseas trip, new car, or entertainment system, for instance, could be selfish rather than just.

So what do we mean when we say just reasons? Being just means thinking and praying about one's responsibility before God and to each other. Married couples must consider what they owe to each other. A husband must attend to the needs of his wife, and she to his. In addition, the couple must consider what they owe to any children they may have. They should also consider their obligations to society. Husband and wife have to decide in their own consciences whether their reasons for delaying children are just. They may ask advice from a priest, friend, or wise person, but they themselves must make the decision. To be clear: couples may use NFP in order to space the conception of their children if there are *just reasons* for doing so, but they should *never* have recourse to artificial methods of contraception.

Pornography, Masturbation, and Oral Sex

The sexual revolution has been compared to a *sewer with many manholes*. Pornography and masturbation are two manholes of that sewer through which sexuality can become degraded. Instead of setting people free, as it should do with husband and wife, sex can become a form of slavery.

Pornography and masturbation represent the destruction of the symbolic and nuptial meaning of the human body. Pornography presents an image focused solely on the visible and the erotic. The human person is reduced to what can be seen. Pornography excludes any sense of the invisible dimension—of the intimacy and sacredness of the human person. Notice, too, that in pornography nobody is there to give and receive. In the world of fantasy it makes, no one is really present.

Thus when a man looks repeatedly at pornography, he will find it difficult to relate to women in real life. He accustoms himself to seeing women as objects to be used. He contents himself with an erotic view of women and thus destroys the symbolic and nuptial meaning of the human body. (The same can be said of a woman who looks at pornography.) In pornography, lust replaces love, and fantasy replaces reality.

Much the same can be said of masturbation. It is an unreal world of fantasy. Notice, however, how masturbation destroys the nuptial meaning of the human body. God gives all men and women erotic energy, which we call the sex drive. This is good, and it forms part of that attraction between men and women that forms part of the nuptial meaning of the body. Sexual energy, therefore, needs to find its outlet in love, not lust.

Erotic energy is meant for another person, in love. If you are a woman, then it is meant for a man, and vice versa. Masturbation turns this erotic energy in on oneself. A person becomes sexually cross-eyed. What is meant for another person, in love, has been turned to the gratification of oneself. Masturbation, therefore, is a symbol of loneliness, not love. One way to overcome it, besides controlling what you read and watch, is to begin to foster genuine friendship with others.

However, the Church, while teaching that masturbation is wrong, also recognizes that a person's guilt for this sin may be reduced because of "immaturity," "acquired habit," certain "conditions of anxiety," or other "psychological or social factors" (*Catechism of the Catholic Church*, no. 2352). These reasons, however, would not excuse the person from the effort to become pure in word and deed. A person's struggle to attain the virtue of purity is pleasing in God's sight, and any form of discouragement should be avoided.

Masturbation is related to oral sex, which for an unmarried couple is a form of mutual masturbation; it becomes the ultimate symbol of using someone for your own pleasure. A married couple cannot use oral sex apart from intercourse, simply as a way to achieve orgasm. But the couple may use it during the foreplay that leads to intercourse. (However, studies have shown that various throat diseases have been linked to oral sex.)

Homosexuality

Homosexuality, or *same-sex attraction*, is not new. But it has become more prominent because of the sexual revolution. We cannot deal with this important topic at length in this book, nor can we deal with the many questions that arise when we broach the topic. A good article to read is "The Origins & Healing of Homosexual Attractions & Behaviors," by Dr. Richard Fitzgibbons. It can be found on the worldwide web.

Perhaps many of us know men and women who have a homosexual orientation. Perhaps they form part of our family. The situation can be very painful indeed, and an open and frank discussion can prove difficult. I will make a few observations here that may be of some help.

Some people choose to be homosexual, while others do not. The two groups should be distinguished. Cardinal George Pell of Sydney, Australia, has said that those who do not choose to be homosexual are *in prisons not of their own making*. That is, there is some cause—cultural and/or familial—beyond the control of the person that disposes them to be attracted to a person of the same sex. The article referred to above is particularly good on this issue.

What may be helpful in trying to reach some clarity is the fact that we are born either male or female, but a task remains ahead for each of us. The task for a male is to develop and cultivate a masculine personality. The task for a female is to develop and cultivate a feminine personality. For various reasons this can prove to be a difficult task. Failure to cultivate the masculine or feminine personality can result in homosexual attraction.

In light of the *Theology of the Body*, we can see that the attraction to someone of the same sex is not part of God's original plan. God intended that men and women would be sexually attracted to each other. Men and women are meant for each other. Their bodies and their persons are complementary. They literally fit together—they become one.

The homosexual person, therefore, is confronted with *two great pains*. First, he or she has the pain of being attracted to a person of the same sex. This real pain causes a feeling of dislocation. In a sense, the person suffers the pain of a lack of personal identity. "Why," asks the homosexual person, "am I attracted to someone of the same sex, when most other people are not?"

Second, the homosexual person has the pain of knowing that homosexual sex can never be a "one-flesh" union. Homosexual sex will never fulfill them. A "one-flesh" union occurs when two people face each other, express their love, and then unite physically. This is impossible in homosexual sex. Two men (or two women) cannot face each other, unite together, and become "one flesh," since their sexual organs cannot be united. This is critically important, for as we have seen, the body is symbolic. The body unites us both physically and spiritually.

The Church teaches, therefore, that the *inclination* to homosexuality is disordered and that *homosexual acts* are sinful. The Church also teaches that this inclination that the homosexual person experiences "constitutes for most of them a trial" (*Catechism of the Catholic Church*, no. 2358). Homosexual persons must strive to live a life of chastity by refraining from homosexual acts. In addition, the Church teaches clearly that homosexual persons "must be accepted with respect, compassion, and sensitivity."

Is there any therapy that will help the homosexual person? Much study and work have taken place in the last twenty years. The article recommended above not only deals with the *causes* of homosexuality, but also documents the *healing* and *therapies* that have been successful in helping homosexual men and women. Becoming aware of this research, based as it is on experience, will give you some wisdom in helping friends who may be experiencing and struggling with same-sex attraction.

> Men and women are meant for each other. Their bodies and their persons are complementary. They literally fit together—they become one.

We should not underestimate the struggle and pain that are part of homosexuality. In our current culture, chastity is difficult. But it is not impossible, for as Jesus told us: "For men this is impossible, but with God all things are possible" (Mt 19:26). Regular prayer, the confession of one's sins, and frequent reception of Christ's body and blood will be a great help in redeeming the body from the trial of homosexuality and struggles with unchastity in general. In addition, persons with homosexual attractions can see their particular difficulties as a cross that is intimately united to the cross of Jesus Christ. Just as Jesus offered up his suffering, so, too, persons with homosexual attractions can offer up their sufferings.

After looking at these various sexual difficulties, we might wonder what happens when we fail sexually. Where do we turn when we find we fall short of the greatness and dignity suggested to us by the *Theology of the Body*? Chapter four deals with this important issue.

Chapter Four

Forgiveness and Trust

We live in an erotic culture. Many television shows, advertisements, magazines, websites, etc., ignore the symbolic nature of the human body. By focusing almost exclusively on the visible dimensions of the human body and thus ignoring the fact that the human body *makes present* the human person, these aspects of culture often portray sex as a fun and easy recreation. This kind of erotic culture ignores the nuptial nature of the human body. Lust, rather than love, reigns supreme in such a sexually saturated environment.

Chastity is difficult. Young people struggle to enter marriage as virgins; married couples struggle to be faithful to each other; men and women struggle to avoid pornography in its many and varied forms. Living the *Theology of the Body* can be difficult. So what can we do?

"Be as Wise as Serpents and Innocent as Doves"

Christ told us to "be as wise as serpents and in-nocent as doves." We need the *wisdom* that comes directly from Christ so we can avoid those places and environments where sex is insulted, belittled, and den-igrated. Likewise, we need to be as *innocent* as doves. Faced with the attraction of illicit sexuality, we need to heed St. Paul's advice and *flee*. In speaking about forni-cation, St. Paul recommended that people *run* from it. We have to try to foresee *where* and *when* we will be tempted to sexual infidelity and avoid those places and times.

The Forgiveness of Jesus Christ

But what do we do if we fail? The answer is simple. We go to Jesus Christ and ask for his mercy. A scene in the Gospel describing the woman taken in adultery can help us understand Jesus' mercy:

> Early in the morning he came again to the temple; all the people came to him, and he sat down and taught them. The scribes and the Pharisees brought *a woman who had been caught in adultery,* and placing her in the midst they said to him, "Teacher, this woman has been caught in the act of adultery. Now in the law Moses commanded us to stone such. What do you say about her?" This they said to test him, that they might

have some charge to bring against him. Jesus bent down and wrote with his finger on the ground. And as they continued to ask him, he stood up and said to them, *"Let him who is without sin among you be the first to throw a stone at her."* And once more he bent down and wrote with his finger on the ground. But when they heard it, they went away, one by one, beginning with the eldest, and Jesus was left alone with the woman standing before him. Jesus looked up and said to her, "Woman, where are they? Has no one condemned you?" She said, "No one, Lord." And Jesus said, *"Neither do I condemn you; go, and do not sin again"* (Jn 8:2–11).

Adultery is a serious matter. It was so serious for the Jews in the Old Testament that if a woman was caught committing it, she would be stoned to death in front of her father's house. Adultery is a betrayal of the marriage covenant and the covenant established with God.

The woman in the Gospel scene was unfaithful, as was the man who engaged in sexual intercourse with her. The people were ready to stone the woman to death. Jesus, full of mercy and understanding, was left alone with her. He forgave her sin and told her never to sin again.

Sexual sin needs to be taken seriously because of who we are. We are temples of the Holy Spirit. But sexual sins are usually *sins of weakness*. They are often not *sins of malice*. If we fail sexually in our lives, then we, too, should go to be alone with Jesus Christ and ask for his mercy. Catholics can go to the sacrament of Reconciliation to confess sins and receive the forgiveness of Jesus Christ.

Pray for this simple faith and for the courage to tell your friends about this splendid reality of Christ's mercy. When we encounter mercy, we will begin to know and love ourselves more deeply. What's more, we will begin to know and love Jesus Christ in a more fruitful and real way.

Trust and the *Theology of the Body*

If we commit sexual sin, we should avoid discouragement. Discouragement is the work of the devil. Jesus Christ has a series of names for the devil. He calls him the *murderer*, the *deceiver*, and the *accuser*. Satan likes to accuse, for he tries to discourage us.

Christ, however, told us that he would send an *Advocate*, that is, someone who is called to our side. This person is the Holy Spirit. The Spirit comes to encourage. Our response should be one of trust.

Trust is critical in all areas of our lives. It is especially important when attempting to understand our sexuality, particularly if we experience failure. Failure can often lead to discouragement. At times it can lead us to question and doubt whether the Church's teachings are true. Repeated failure can lead us to think that perhaps the Church is not correct. Might not the *Theology of the Body* be fine in a perfect world, but hardly practical in the twenty-first century? Can we really embrace and live it?

Here the principle of trust is important. There can be little doubt that John Paul II has given us something entirely fresh and attractive. Still, as I noted in the introduction, our sexuality is a paradox. It is a wonderful gift, but the difficulties encountered can cause problems of trust.

A thought from St. Augustine might be helpful. He once said that "we believe in order to understand; we don't understand in order to believe." This insight can be applied to the human body and sexuality. Let me explain with an example.

In Australia in 1998 there was a celebration marking the thirtieth anniversary of *Humanae Vitae*, the papal document that had caused a storm by affirming the Church's opposition to contraception. Some people were in favor of the celebration, but quite a few people were not. I was very impressed by a letter I received from a woman who was in her early twenties back in 1968. She said that when Pope Paul VI published *Humanae Vitae*, she was angry. But she said, "My husband and I trusted the pope." They decided to follow what he taught. Thirty years later this woman was glad that they did. By believing and living it, she came to understand its value.

The point is this. The Church's teachings on the human body and sex are like the other teachings of the Church. The teachings are reasonable, and the mind can grasp them. But their prime target is the human heart. In other words, they are teachings that you have *to live in order to understand*. The meaning of a mystery of faith comes to light when we begin to live what it means. Our lives, not so much our minds, are the real interpreters of doctrines.

> The meaning of a mystery of faith comes to light when we begin to live what it means.

Simone Weil, a prominent Jewish writer, has noted that the Old Testament is shot through with this idea: *we recognize good by doing it; we recognize evil by not doing it.* We recognize the goodness of the commandment to "love one another" by actually helping and serving people. On the other hand, we recognize the evil of talking behind people's back when we make a conscious effort to be merciful toward others.

Likewise, we will come to recognize the truth and beauty of the Church's sexual teaching by trying to live it. And we will come to a vivid awareness of the evil of adultery, for instance, by being faithful in marriage.

The *Theology of the Body*, with its four original experiences, therefore, will help us to travel the path of goodness. We will come to recognize, through our experiences, the goodness and beauty of our human bodies. And we will come to acknowledge the goodness and beauty of the relationships that form the very essence of our lives.

BOOKS & MEDIA

The Daughters of St. Paul operate book and media centers at the following addresses. Visit, call or write the one nearest you today, or find us on the World Wide Web, www.pauline.org

CALIFORNIA

3908 Sepulveda Blvd, Culver City, CA 90230	310-397-8676
5945 Balboa Avenue, San Diego, CA 92111	858-565-9181
2640 Broadway Street, Redwood City, CA 94063	650-369-4230

FLORIDA

145 S.W. 107th Avenue, Miami, FL 33174	305-559-6715

HAWAII

1143 Bishop Street, Honolulu, HI 96813	808-521-2731
Neighbor Islands call:	866-521-2731

ILLINOIS

172 North Michigan Avenue, Chicago, IL 60601	312-346-4228

LOUISIANA

4403 Veterans Memorial Blvd, Metairie, LA 70006	504-887-7631

MASSACHUSETTS

885 Providence Hwy, Dedham, MA 02026	781-326-5385

MISSOURI

9804 Watson Road, St. Louis, MO 63126	314-965-3512

NEW JERSEY

561 U.S. Route 1, Wick Plaza, Edison, NJ 08817	732-572-1200

NEW YORK

150 East 52nd Street, New York, NY 10022	212-754-1110

PENNSYLVANIA

9171-A Roosevelt Blvd, Philadelphia, PA 19114	215-676-9494

SOUTH CAROLINA

243 King Street, Charleston, SC 29401	843-577-0175

TENNESSEE

4811 Poplar Avenue, Memphis, TN 38117	901-761-2987

TEXAS

114 Main Plaza, San Antonio, TX 78205	210-224-8101

VIRGINIA

1025 King Street, Alexandria, VA 22314	703-549-3806

CANADA

3022 Dufferin Street, Toronto, ON M6B 3T5	416-781-9131

Other Resources from Pauline Books & Media

The Theology of the Body
A New Translation Based on the John Paul II Archives

John Paul II

A recent discovery in Rome's John Paul II Archives proved to be the pope's original manuscript of *Theology of the Body*, with John Paul's handwritten notes and his own division of the text, a division which had been previously altered by editors and which offers the interpretive key to unlocking the work. This material, together with a long-awaited new translation of the original text, makes this new release of John Paul II's *The Theology of the Body* the critical edition, and the foundation for all future work in this area.

Theology of the Body presents John Paul II's magnificent vision of the human person, understood within the mystery of Christ. Going back to the biblical "beginning" as recorded in Genesis, the pope discusses the bodily dimension of human personhood, sexuality, and marriage in the light of biblical revelation. Beginning with three primordial human experiences—original solitude, original unity and original nakedness—John Paul outlines the spousal meaning of the body, reflects on the communion of persons, considers chastity for the sake of the Kingdom, and discusses the "language of the body" with regard to contraception.

Accompanying this new translation is an extensive introduction, an extensive glossar,y and a complete index.

Introduction, translation, and editing by Dr. Michael
Waldstein, International Theological Institute for Studies on
Marriage and the Family in Gaming, Austria.

Foreword by Christopher West.

ISBN 0-8198-7421-3

The Theology of the Body Explained

A Commentary on John Paul II's "Gospel of the Body"

Christopher West

A clear and profound commentary on Pope John Paul II's
Theology of the Body, which "breaks open" the Holy Father's
thought regarding the human person and sexuality.

Paperback   552pp.   0-8198-7410-8 $29.95

God's Plan for You

Life, Love, Marriage, and Sex

By David Hajduk

Have you ever wondered what life is all about? Ever struggled
with finding your place in this world? Have you ever looked in
the mirror and not been sure if you like what you see, or even
know what you see? Ever been confused about relationships,
sex, or members of the opposite sex? Are you disillusioned
about marriage and family life? Well, you're not alone.

Living in the information age, it's surprising how hard it
can be to find the answers to important life questions. We are

bombarded on all sides with contradictory images from our parents, Church leaders, celebrities, and society—it's hard to know what to believe about anything.

God's Plan for You, based on John Paul II's *Theology of the Body*, offers a path that will lead to a full life and a reason to hope for the future. In this book, David Hajduk makes John Paul II's magnificent vision of the human person accessible to today's youth. Delve into this vision to discover the purpose of existence and the answers to your most deeply held questions about life, relationships, and sexuality.

Softcover   208pp.   0-8198-4517-5

Of Human Life

Humanae Vitae

Pope Paul VI

July 25, 1968

On the regulation of birth.

Softcover   16pp.   0-8198-3347-9 $1.25

The Gospel of Life

Evangelium Vitae

Pope John Paul II

March 25, 1995

On the value and inviolability of human life.

Softcover   176pp.   0-8198-3078-X $6.95

God Is Love

Deus Caritas Est

Pope Benedict XVI

December 25, 2005

The Encyclical is divided into two long parts. The first presents a theological-philosophical reflection on "love" in its various dimensions—"eros," "philia," and "agape"—highlighting certain vital aspects of God's love for man and the inherent links that such love has with human love. The second part concerns the concrete implementation of the commandment to love others.

Softcover   64pp.   0-8198-3106-9 $6.95